Just Us by Nobody

Randolph Lancaster

The Reading Glass Books
1-888-420-3050
www.readingglassbooks.com
production@readingglassbooks.com

Just Us by Nobody

I'm writing this book because I'm old, and I'm broke, and I think now is the time to write it. Partially I'm writing it now because of what I see going on in this country with law and order. The system isn't getting better, it's getting worse.

I'm writing this book to tell people what it's really like to be caught up in the legal system. To be dehumanized and humiliated by those in a position of power. Life inside the prison system is one of our country's many "dirty little secrets". Except in the case of the prison system, the problem is pretty damn big.

I was born in Topeka, Kansas in 1948. My mother was quite a bit younger than my father, which was common around that time. When I was born my father was 47 and my mother was 24, and I was her fourth child! My sister Dee was the oldest and I had two older brothers, Jack and Don.

My mother and father were divorced in 1950, which wasn't so common back then. After the divorce, Dee and I went with my mother and Jack and Don stayed with my father, although I think they would've rather come with us. My mother eventually remarried, this time to her sister's ex-husband Clifford. Before leaving Clifford, her sister Mary had given birth to four children who all continued to live with their mother. So as a result of the strange twisting of our family tree, I had 3 stepsisters and a step-brother, who were also my cousins!

In 1955 the four of us moved to Colorado. We lived in an old neighborhood called Globeville, and I went to school at York Street Elementary under the viaducts near Denver's stock show complex. The York Street playground in the summer was all sizzling blacktop, surrounded by chain-link fence that was topped with barbed-wire.

We didn't live there long. Less than a year later we moved a few miles away to Commerce City. I went to 1st grade at Adams City Elementary and then we moved again I went to Monaco Elementary for 2nd grade. During this time, my stepfather Clifford was starting to become abusive, and he would regularly beat me as punishment for the smallest mistake.

When I was in 2nd grade, I got bit by a stray dog that wandered onto the playground during recess. I was taken to the office where two teachers lifted my shirt to examine the dog bite and saw the welts on my back that ran all the way to the tops of my shoulders. Welts left from where my stepfather had beaten me and whipped me with his belt. One teacher suggested that they report the injuries to the authorities, but the other teacher quickly said, "No, he would get it worse if we reported it." They knew about the abuse going on at my house and were worried that my stepfather might retaliate if he was accused. So they didn't report it and the abuse continued. I often wonder what would've happened if they had reported the abuse. Things may have turned out differently.

School for me was an escape from what was going on at home. When I was at school, I would stare out the window and daydream about my original family. I desperately wanted to be reunited with my father and my brothers.

Dee wanted to get out of that situation as badly as I did and she got married young. She married a guy in the service which worked out well. They eventually had 2 girls and 2 boys and had a pretty good life.

I hated Clifford, but I loved my mother. I didn't see what she saw in him - maybe it was security, or just his ability to provide. Whatever she was getting out of the marriage, it didn't seem worth the suffering that was being inflicted on me.

Clifford not only beat me like a dog, he also worked me like one. Clifford was in the salvage business and every day he would go to machine shops, garages, and junkyards to buy up scrap aluminum; then he would go to plumbing shops for copper and brass. The metal had to be cleaned before he could resell it, so I was given the task of cleaning the dirt and rust off salvaged metal. It was brutal, exhausting work and for my labor I never received so much as one red cent. The beatings quit around the 4th grade, but after that Clifford would get his ounce of flesh though my labor.

Every day after school I would change my clothes, go out to the shed, and start in on a pile of rusty junk metal. I spent hours a day cleaning; fighting with all my adolescent strength to dislodge stuck bolts from aluminum pistons. Even though the work was tedious and difficult, I realized that I was developing a love and appreciation for the inner working of automobiles. I didn't know it at the time, but this love and knowledge of cars would end up starting me down the road of juvenile delinquency.

In 5th grade I had one of the best teachers I can remember, Mr. Zietlow. It was the first time I really felt motivated to do well in school and show my teacher that I could make the grade. Unfortunately, I still wasn't getting any support at home and while I worked on my homework, my parents would watch me, staring at me with confused expressions. My mother and Clifford had only reached the 8th grade and didn't know what to think when I decided to be a good student. When I was stuck on a particularly difficult arithmetic problem, my mother said I should just ask one of the other students for the answer. I told her, "The right answer isn't enough." I explained that I had to show my work and demonstrate how I came to the right answer. Mr. Zeitlow was the kind of teacher that made you want to do the work and not just crib answers off another kid's paper.

When I went to Kerney Jr. High, I had a 7th grade teacher named Mr. Karsic. Think of Doc Brown in Back to the Future. He didn't look like him really, but he was a geek and he was always geeking out before geeks or geeking out was a thing. I guess what I mean is that he was always really passionate about what he was teaching. And sometimes he took it a bit overboard.

One day while I was in English class, the whole school had to be evacuated to the football field. We were all standing on the field, buzzing with the excitement that comes from being pulled out of class unexpectedly. I eventually ran into a classmate friend and asked why we were out there. He told me Mr. Krasic, in the course of a classroom experiment, had created a chemical reaction that stunk up the whole school with Sulphur gas.

It probably goes without saying, but it was very different growing up in the 50s and 60s than it is now. At that time, you could buy baby alligators at the pet store for a dollar. It was, on average, a pretty cruel process. None of the children that bought one of the reptiles could keep them alive for more than a few days. But Mr. Krasic told us he could not only keep them alive, but get them to grow, and he did just that. Eventually the gator he raised got to be so big that the school district told him he had to get rid of it. The students were of course sad that they wouldn't go to the school and see the alligator, but they were still able to see it when they visited the Denver Zoo.

When I was 14, I got my first real job at the historic Elitch's Gardens Amusement Park in the Denver suburbs. I rode an old motor-scooter that I'd fixed up and got pretty good at weaving between the traffic on my ride to work and back. When I turned 16, I got a my first car: a 1955 Chevy that cost me $125.

Over the course of my teenage years, I'd be surprised if I said a thousand words to my mother and Clifford. I hated Clifford's guts, and for some reason, when I was 16, the universe saw fit to test how deep that hatred ran.

It was fall and Clifford had dragged me along on a deer hunting trip. We were hiking down the side of a mountain, Clifford leading the way, carefully picking his footsteps across the rocky terrain when he stopped dead in his tracks. Directly to his right was a rock ledge and on the ledge was a rattlesnake, coiled in a tight ball and loudly rattling its tail. I slowly moved toward him and saw that the snake was about 4 feet from his head.

I quickly yanked my gun sling, pulling my 300 Savage Rifle over my shoulder and took aim at the snake as quickly as I could. I shot it twice, although the first shot probably did the trick. Before I shot, I

4

told Clifford to turn his head away in case the bullet ricocheted off the rocks, and I wonder if he thought that I might take the chance to shoot him.

There was no person who I hated more in the world at that moment than Clifford, but that didn't mean that I had it in me to murder him in cold blood.

Only a few months later I was helping Clifford in the garage when a jack slipped, almost crushing him under the weight of a car. Trapped under the car's rear bumper, Clifford struggled to breathe as I found another jack and lifted the car off of him. He ended up with a couple of cracked ribs. Once again life had placed me in a situation that put my humanity to the test. Fortunately for Clifford, he had received more humane treatment than he'd ever offered me in return.

By the time I was 16, my career as a petty criminal was beginning to take shape. I could hotwire a car with a chewing gum wrapper. And with a six-inch piece of copper wire and two alligator clips, I could bypass most alarms. Of course, with my first crimes came my first encounters with the law.

The first time I was busted, I ended up getting probation for what we called "midnight auto supply." In those days, new cars were brought in on the train and dropped off on Quebec street near the old Stapleton Airport. There wasn't any security, just a big parking lot full of new cars, protected by nothing but a chain-link fence.

Our main targets were the spare tires in the cars' trunks – easy to get out of the car and easy to find a buyer at a shady auto parts dealer. It was especially easy when they didn't even lock the cars, just left two keys sitting in the ashtray. Man, it was a different time. All you had to do was act the part. We would wear work clothes and move quickly and intentionally, like we had a job to do. Which we did, just not a legal one.

Then, as a cherry on top of the sundae, we would siphon gas from a car to get the fuel we needed to leave the scene. In those days it was pretty common to have cars that ran on diesel fuel and one time a friend of mine accidentally siphoned diesel gas into a car that ran on regular. When he tried to start it up the car gave off a sound like a metallic burp and started shooting black smoke from the exhaust pipe. A few seconds later smoke started coming from under the hood and the guy ditched the car and jumped in with us as we left.

On Larimer Street back in the day you could sell pretty much anything, whether it was acquired legally or illegally. The folks who were buying my tires knew they were stolen, but they weren't so prim and proper as to turn away a good deal.

Along with tires, I used to do a fair amount of business in hubcaps. In those days fancy hubcaps were one of the flashiest accessories for a car...and also one of the easiest to steal. I would look for the top-of-the-line hubcaps - three bar spinners, four bar spinners, beauty rims, baby moons – and take them down to Hubcap Annie's. It was a national chain of auto parts stores but they still bought my stolen merchandise. (That Hubcap Annie's location on Larimer finally got busted in the mid 80s after a few decades of being an active participant in Denver's auto parts black market.)

When I got arrested the first time, I was working at the Denver Theater, at 15th and Glenarm. Cat Baloo was the big show back in the day. That and James Bond movies. I stood at the entrance to the theater and said the same thing over-and-over as customers walked through the doors: "Good evening, Going in now? Please use the stairway to the right for your balcony seats and aisles 1 and 2 on the main floor or whatever other seating is available. Thank you." I was actually on the clock when the cops showed up looking for me.

It turns out an acquaintance of mine from high school had gotten picked up for stealing tires and ratted out anyone he could. The cops showed up at the theater, dragged me out to their squad car and took me straight to juvenile hall on Downing Street. That was my first time locked up, but it wouldn't be a long first stretch. My folks came down and bailed me out the next day.

In 1965, at the age of 17, I left home and went to Kansas with my brother. Our plan was to move back in with our father and to help with our resettlement, we'd stolen some band instruments from a junior high school in Denver that we planned to sell in Kansas. Our cousin, Gerald Robinson, was another up-and-coming crook who was going to help us fence the goods.

We'd crossed over the state line into the Missouri side where we found a pawn shop that we hoped would buy the instruments, but apparently they'd gotten word of the stolen instruments. After we'd left the shop, they called the police. We had just crossed the bridge back into Kansas when we got picked up for a crime we'd committed back in Colorado. I guess that's what they mean by the 'long arm of the law'

We were arrested in Kansas City and taken back to Topeka where we were booked in for burglary. It was my first time actually behind bars. This time I wasn't put in juvenile hall. In fact, I was so close to being an adult that they kept me in pretrial detention until my 18th birthday and then tried me as an adult. I got six months followed by a year of probation. This wasn't a one night stint in juvie, this was real time.

I was serving the time with my brother and our cousin Gerald. A couple months into our sentence, Gerald was getting restless and started hatching a plan to escape. My role was to cut up bedsheets and tie them together end-to-end to make a rope. Another inmate, Jesse Phillips, had stolen a pair of shears from the shop that would be used to cut the metal security screen from a window on the third floor. The plan was that Gerald and an elderly guy named Loren would get lowed into the yard with the rope where they would crawl under the gate and onto freedom.

Loren went first and we slowly lowered him down, watching him fade into the darkness with the sheets tied around his waist. He made it to the ground without any issues and we pulled to rope back up to the top. Gerald tied the rope around his waist, crawled through the jagged edges of the cut security screen and out into the dark. He was about halfway down when the sheets broke, and all we heard was a thud when he hit the ground. He must've tried real hard not to yell out.

I guess no guards were alerted by the men escaping since it wasn't until the next morning when they discovered that Gerald and Loren weren't in their cells. The two of them were on the lam about three weeks before they were eventually arrested. After he got caught, Gerald was resentenced and sent to Hutchison Prison for an additional 14 months. He traded three weeks of freedom – if you want to call it that – for almost a year of his life.

After serving my time for stealing the band instruments, I got out of jail in 1967. My time in jail had only made me more familiar with crime and criminals, so it wasn't long until I ended up back inside the system.

What happened was I'd gone to a party with some of my friends of mine in Topeka, Kansas on California Avenue. I met a girl at the party and while we were fooling around my friends went across the street and broke into a liquor store. They were already shitfaced, but they'd run out of booze and decided to cause a little mayhem while they restocked.

My friend Harvey went in first; he busted out the door with a hatchet and crawled in through the broken glass. They grabbed armfuls of bottles, breaking their fair share along the way, and before long George shouted that the police were coming. Harvey wasn't so careful on the way out of the store and jumped through the plate glass window, giving him a deep cut that ran almost the whole length of his bicep. And the funny part? The police weren't even coming.

For the record I never went into the liquor store, I just watched them come back from across the street. But that didn't matter. The police found out I was a witness to the crime and being an accessory to the crime was a violation of my probation.

I was living with my dad at the time on the outskirts of Topeka, the boonies as we called it. We lived north-east of the city on Kinkaid road where it came to a dead end. My aunt and uncle owned a salvage yard and my dad had his mobile home back there. I'd been working for a couple named the Fairchilds, taking odd shifts on their garbage truck, and a couple days after the liquor store robbery they tipped me off that the police were looking for me.

I felt like a sitting duck at my dad's place, stuck at the end of the road with only one way out. My '57 Ford was the only way to get out of dodge, but the car had a busted starter. I knew if I got it going, I could drive over to one of the garages in town where I did business and get it fixed up. And like I said before, I could get a car going with just about anything. It took a few minutes, but I eventually got the car started and was on my way up Kinkaid Road, happy to be putting distance between me and that mobile home. I figured after I got my car fixed, I'd head to a friend's house to lay low.

The police were waiting for me at the end of the road. Three cars parked behind some trees so I couldn't see them until the last minute. I gunned it through the intersection, throwing up a cloud of dirt and dust behind me, and drove toward Topeka, blowing through all the stop signs on the way into the city. I was doing 65 mph through downtown, weaving between late afternoon traffic. One of the cops was right on my tail and tried to weave into the side of my car; a PIT maneuver. He missed his target, weaving across a lane of traffic and crashing into a row of parking meters.

I felt like I was gaining some distance now. I took a hard left, the car's tires squealing as the back end swung out and right then the car died. Right in the middle of my escape the car was dead and I couldn't restart it because it didn't have a starter. I took off on foot and started climbing up a nearby fire escape when an officer put his flashlight on me. I knew that the jig was up and slowly climbed down the fire escape to face the music.

After all was said and done, the police compared notes and wrote me 52 traffic tickets for my role in the chase and took me down to jail to await my trial. I found out after my arrest that the cop who hit the parking meters had broken his leg in the crash, so that didn't help my case. After a few days I had my first hearing for the traffic tickets, in the courtroom of the honorable Judge Robine, who happened to be blind. I guess he kind of embodied that old cliché about the justice system.

When they read the laundry list of my charges I couldn't help but laugh. Not only was the list of citations hilariously long, but the whole situation was ridiculous. The judge, annoyed with my laughing, asked the district attorney what was going on and he told the judge that I wasn't worried about the misdemeanor charges... because I was facing felony charges upstairs for the violation of my probation during the liquor store robbery. The judge didn't think it was as funny as I did, but he agreed that it didn't make sense to punish me for the misdemeanors with my outstanding felony arrest, so the charges were dismissed.

Even in those days, the wheels of justice moved very slowly and my felony case took a lot longer to sort out than the misdemeanor. I had to wait another six months for a decision while I was sitting in jail. The state was threatening me with two sentences of 5 to 10, one for the probation violation and one for the accessory charge. And the DA said if I took this case to court they would push for the sentences to run consecutive to each other. So I would have had to serve one 5 to 10 and then serve the other 5 to 10 afterward. This was enough to convince me to take the plea deal and in exchange they agreed to have my sentences served concurrently.

It may sound crazy, but I would rather be rich and guilty any day then poor and innocent. Why? In a very real way, money buys you freedom. If I'd come from money, I would've gotten out on bond and lived as a free man until I was found guilty. The bond system back then, just like the cash bail system today, was used as a tool to get leverage against defendants and as an opportunity for the ones running the system to line their own pockets. If you didn't make bond they had a year to take your case to trial. In other words, they would have a year to postpone your defense while you rot away in jail. A year of your life before you've even been found guilty.

Kidwell

While I was in jail in 1968, awaiting a trial that would never happen, there was a lot of talk going around about a guy named Kidwell. He'd been a legislator for the State of Kansas, but I'd never heard of him. Kidwell was accused of killing his wife Betty, who he'd married a year earlier in Reno, Nevada.

As far as the police could tell, he shot Betty while they were inside their Cadillac and then he drove away with her body still in the car. About an hour later, he crashed the car into a ditch on a dirt road southeast of Topeka, where someone called it in. When the police arrived, 43 year-old Thomas Kidwell was slumped over the steering wheel, shot twice in the chest, still alive. Betty's body was on the floor, nude except for a necklace and earrings, shot four times through the heart.

The pistol that would eventually be connected to all the bullets was found on the front seat of the car and the going theory was that it was a murder/suicide gone wrong. After getting medical attention, Kidwell was charged with 1st degree murder, but got out on bond.

This was a big case in the state and was making headlines in all the newspapers. Everybody in jail said he would get out with very little time, but I was holding out hope that the justice system would be fair. I'm not a lawyer, but I know that the law doesn't mean squat if it doesn't get applied to everyone equally.

Kidwell's first trial lasted all of one week. The jury found him guilty and recommended a life sentence. Life at that time was Life - no parole. The only way to get out was clemency by the Governor and the odds of that happening were like winning the lottery, except worse. Kidwell's attorney immediately appealed the decision and he was granted a new trial. The appeal process would drag on through most of 1967, leaving Kidwell a free man. He took advantage of that freedom by marrying his third wife - after having just been found guilty of murdering his second wife.

I didn't know about all of this in 1967, when I was sitting in jail waiting for a verdict on my parole violation. I knew about a guy called Kidwell and that his case was all over the news, but I figured he was just another rich guy that would never end up in the can with us rabble. Turns out I was only half right about that one.

Kidwell's first trial made headlines in Kansas, but his second trial would be written up in the national press. Time Magazine published an article on the trial in December of 1967 with the headline, 'Reliving a Murder'. It described Kidwell's crime as, "...the murder of his promiscuous wife..." and added the detail that Kidwell had apparently had sex with his wife in the car either before or after she was murdered.

This is where it gets really interesting. As the Time article describes it, "the essential ingredient [at the second trial] was something new—an hour-long video tape of Kidwell reliving the murder under the influence of a drug." This was only the second time video tape had been used as evidence during a trial in the US, and Kidwell's lawyers were hoping that what was on this tape would convince the judge and prosecution to reduce or overturn his sentence.

The tape showed Kidwell under the influence of Sodium Amobarbital – a kind of 'truth serum' that had been used unsuccessfully to treat soldiers with shell shock. This was the 60s and everybody was talking about mind control and Manchurian Candidates, so I guess it's not too surprising that the judge allowed this kind of evidence to be presented at the trial, but that isn't the kind of thing that happens if you can't afford a good lawyer.

In the video, a psychiatrist instructs Kidwell to relive the experience of killing his wife. Kidwell recalls, in slurred speech, having an argument with her and then the video shows him recoil in physical pain, as if he'd been shot. "Finally, his jumbled words conveyed that he had got the gun and shot her," according to the Time reporter. This new version of the murder reversed the order of the shooting, casting Kidwell as the victim who murdered his wife in self-defense.

I don't know if Kidwell was telling the truth on that video or if it was some elaborate stunt, but it sounded like a bunch of bullshit. The video evidence wasn't enough to get Kidwell off entirely, but it gave his legal team enough leverage to have his charge reduced from murder to manslaughter and have his sentence dropped from life to 5 to 21 years.

After pleading guilty to first-degree manslaughter, Kidwell was taken to KRDC - the Kansas Reception and Diagnostic Center. This is where our paths would cross for the first time. Inmates couldn't leave KRDC, but it didn't feel as much like a jail, more like a high security hospital. Most prisoners were at KRDC for one week – going through battery of physical and psychological tests – before they were sent to prison, but Kidwell had already been there a month when I arrived. All the convicts that I knew had to wait in jail between their conviction and sentencing, but Kidwell got to bypass jail altogether. That pissed me off to not end, but I figured he'd end up in prison just like the rest of us and I took some comfort from that thought.

Arriving to Lansing

We went to Lansing Prison on a big blue bus on a day that was cold and rainy. It was a full-size bus, but there were only 4 of us riding to prison. It was a miserable day. When you come up to the front of the Kansas State Penitentiary in Lansing, it felt like an old medieval castle with massive grey walls that looked as cold and dreary as the weather. The year I arrived, Lansing turned 100 years-old, and it looked every day of it.

To get to Receiving and Discharge we entered through the main gate, which I would come to learn is the Administration Building, and then we proceeded through four more gates. The Administration Building was also called Tower 13 and served as the offices for the men that would dictate how we lived our lives.

At Receiving and Discharge we were each given a small fabric bag. The bag contained one bar of soap, a box of tooth powder (not paste), a toothbrush, and one very old and used set of headphones that would allow us to listen to music from a radio transmitter that was built into the wall in each cell. There was KPRS out of Kansas City, Rock and Roll out of Topeka, and Country and Western from somewhere else. You were also issued one wool blanket, two sheets, and a pillowcase.

After we were done at the Receiving and Discharge area, everyone except for Kidwell was taken to quarantine. He was escorted by a guard to Protective Custody (PC). PC is what most people know as 'the hole'. It was a dank, cramped cell where you were held for 23 hours out of the day. Normally, the people that end up in PC were being punished for breaking the prison rules, but Kidwell was put in the hole because he was scared, and this was a way for him to be protected from the general population. In his case, protective custody wasn't a euphemism, it was 100% accurate.

We were held in quarantine for a week. Before going to our cells, we were led to Central Bath, located underneath C Cell House. We came down a narrow stairway and into a long white hallway. From a small room to the left we got our boots, which we called 'brogans'. (I noticed that the soles of the boots had a V-shaped notch cut into the tread. I would learn later that this was to help the authorities in tracking the footprints of escaped convicts.) Further down the hall we came to a room where we were issued 3 pairs of pants, 3 shirts, and 3 pairs of underwear; your name and prison number stamped on all of it.

When we finally got to the showers, I went around a long wall that had 3 bathing areas with 30 showerheads in each one. It was an enormous area with no privacy for anyone. Along the other side of the wall across from the shower stalls was a wall with a long bench, about 50 feet from end-to-end. It was one of the biggest rooms I'd ever seen.

After clearing quarantine, I got my first look at the prison yard. I stopped a moment and took stock of my surroundings. I had just turned 19 and would now have to learn to live in "The Devil's Backyard", the nickname prisoners had given to Lansing. Because of the fact that I had been in and out of the system, I made friends pretty quickly. If I had one advantage in prison, it was being pretty comfortable associating with other criminals.

Since I had some friends and acquaintances that were already locked up at Lansing, I was allowed to request placement in a specific cell. I filled out a form when I was being processed and then when I arrived to the cell block, I already had a reservation!

My roommates were Nick, Edgar, John, and Catfish. They had agreed to let me take one of the empty bunks in their 6-man cell. Nick, we called "Nick the Greek" because he was a big gambler and ran a poker game on the yard. Edgar and I had met in jail a year before when I was in for stealing the band instruments and John was Edgar's cousin. Catfish was released a month or so after I arrived. Not long after getting out, he was killed in a bar fight in Oklahoma. I heard he pulled a knife on a guy, and the other guy pulled out a gun.

Word of what had happened with Kidwell was already getting around. I'd come to find out that the prisoners at Lansing almost always knew when someone what getting preferential treatment. As they say, there's no honor among thieves, but there is some solidarity among inmates.

My cellmates told me we were locked down in our cells every day at 4pm and couldn't leave until 7am the next morning. They also told me that "the count" happened every day at 4pm. Prisoners had to stand in their cells while guards walked each level, counting heads and locking doors. I thought it was pretty demeaning that we had to stand at attention, but I didn't want to stick my neck out.

After living there for a few days, we heard that Kidwell was living in a brand-new mobile home next to the Warden's house and working in the Administration Office with the warden's secretary. He was allowed to come and go from the main administration office to his mobile home like it was nothing. No security guard, no escort, nothing. We were dumfounded. We were in the Devil's Backyard, and he was outside the walls, living in blissful ignorance of all the shit on the inside.

Now everyone understood the anger I was feeling over Kidwell. The day after we found out about his preferential treatment, every prisoner in C Cell House refused to stand for the count. We risked getting a beating to make a point about this bullshit, "laws for thee and not for me" system. The protest was only partially successful: Kidwell went on living his charmed life, but we never had to stand for the count against as long as I was there. It was good to see that the inmates at Lansing stood for something, even if it sometimes felt like it was every man for himself.

<u>Early Days at Lansing</u>

Soon after arriving at the prison, I got a job in the Tag Factory making license plates. License plates that would end up on the car of some average Joe who never gave a second thought to who was making them. The work wasn't too hard, and I made friends pretty quick with another factory worker named John. He'd already been there for 5 or 6 years and, looking back on it now, I was lucky to meet a guy like that who kind of showed me the ropes and helped me survive that first year in Lansing.

One rainy day on the way back from the tag factory to C Cell Block, we passed by this guy named Red, He shouts out, "I'll kill you Elizabeth!" I was new to prison and that kind of spooked me. My name wasn't Elizabeth, but neither was anyone else's in the joint and I was standing closest to the guy so I figured he was talking to me. I turned to John and said, "What the hell is he talking about?!"

"Don't worry about it. He killed Elizabeth 20 years ago." John said. It might have been kind of funny if I hadn't been imagining that this crazy guy was about to kill me thinking I was someone named Elizabeth! There were with a lot of guys with a screw loose in prison. Some were like that when they got there, and some lose it while they're inside. Being locked up for a long time will do that to a person.

John was real prison encyclopedia and could tell you stories about pretty much anybody. Information is like money in prison so it's good to be a guy who knows things. There was an older guy in our cell block that everyone called "Smoothie". He didn't seem particularly smooth to me so I asked John, "Why do they call him Smoothie?"

"He worked in the Carpenter shop and didn't know what a plane was." John said. "So he asked somebody, 'Hand me that smoother?' Everyone in the shop lost it at that, and laughed their asses off. And so they just started calling him Smoothie from then on." I'd find out that pretty much everybody ended up getting a nickname in prison one way or another. Well, except for me. Oddly enough I never picked up a nickname, at least not one that stuck.

Another story I heard from John was about the time Smoothie and some other guys tried to break out. The leader of the group wasn't Smoothie, but a guy called Tar and he had a plan to escape through Tower 13. It wasn't exactly a secret route. Tower 13 was the main entrance to the prison!

They would also have to go through four gates before they got out. Tar's plan? Take a hostage and negotiate their way to freedom. They ended up overpowering one of the guards at the first gate. A guy named Kanege. They got as far as the last gate, but the warden held the line and wouldn't let them out of the prison. Tar told the Warden, "I'm gonna' kill this motherfucker if you don't open the gate." The warden refused. If he had known Tar better, he might've made a different call. Tar killed the guard on the spot, stabbed him to death. I don't know why the warden didn't just let them out, I'm sure they would've gotten caught soon enough, but he wasn't willing to budge, and it cost Kanege his life.

It wouldn't take long until Tar followed his victim to the prison morgue. It was just a couple months after I arrived, about 6 months after the attempted escape, and it was the type of thing I wouldn't ever forget.

You might assume that Tar was killed by the guards in retaliation for what he did to Kanege, but it turned out there were a lot of people who wanted to take revenge on him.

I worked with Tar in the Tag Factory. I'm not a small man but standing next to Tar I felt like I was 'knee-high to a grasshopper' as my dad and his generation used to say. And he wasn't just tall, he was burly. Even at 40-something, he could drop down and do a hundred push-ups without breaking a sweat. But I didn't like Tar. I wouldn't say we were enemies - he had enough of those already – but I didn't like him. Nobody liked him.

Having enemies on the outside is bad enough, but at least you might have a place to hide. On the inside, unless you're in protective custody or solitary, you're all fish swimming in the same small pond. Even for the biggest, most intimidating guy in the prison, having enemies was bound to catch up with him eventually. These two guys Butch and Terry had a beef with Tar over some stolen leatherworking tools. They knew it was just a matter of time before Tar tried to get back at them, so they made up their minds to strike first.

Butch and Terry smuggled a bucket of gas and paint remover from the prison garage back to the cell block. They also found a length of chain and when Tar was sleeping, they wrapped the chain around the bars, so that even the guards wouldn't be able to get him out. Butch got to dumping the gas into the cell while Terry produced a matchbook from the pocket of his jeans and WHOOSH! That prison cell went off like a fireball and you could just see the outlines of Terry and Butch against the light from the fire. They were already hotfooting it out of there.

Tar eventually walked out of his cell, but it took some time. Too much time for a man engulfed in flames, that's for damn sure. It was night and the guards didn't have a way to break through the locked chain, so they sent a couple guys to the vocational shop to get bolt cutters. By the time they got the cell open they'd mostly put out the flames, but Tar was burnt to the point where we could see his flesh falling off in chunks as he tried to walk. The craziest part? He didn't say a word through the whole thing. Didn't make a sound. They took him to the hospital inside of the prison and he was apparently able give the names of Butch and Terry as the perpetrators. Tar ended up dying that same night. Eventually they convicted Butch for the murder, but not Terry. It turns out that because there were other Terrys in prison at the same time, and Tar only gave the one name, they couldn't prove it was him. Butch never gave him up and Terry got away with murder. Life in prison can sometime have a sick sense of humor that way.

The prison doctors couldn't save Tar, which didn't surprise anybody, he was messed up. Butch and Terry turned his cell into a giant oven and cooked him alive. But you didn't need to be burned alive in your cell to die in the prison hospital, you could easily die from something minor.

One day on the way out of Chow Hall, John and I saw a big crowd gathering in front of the hospital. We walked over there to see what was going on and someone told us it was about Herman, an inmate who had just had his tonsils removed. The medical staff were supposed to be monitoring him during his recovery, but no one did and he died from an infection. Herman was a black man, and maybe that had something to do with it, but as inmates we felt like it couldn't have happened to any of us, black or white. They just didn't give a shit about us.

But now they had to give a shit. Now there was a mob forming outside of the hospital. The fact that it was Herman who had died was like salt in the wound. He was one of the most well-liked guys in the whole place and could tell a joke to put a smile on your face even in the darkest times. In other words, he was a good man and a rare man in Lansing Prison.

My cellmate Nick was in the front of the crowd, pushing against a sea of bodies to try and get up closer to the warden and the prison guards who stood on the steps of the hospital. Nick reached the front of the mob and moved up the steps until he was face-to-face with Warden Wilson. He wasn't there for more than a moment before Nick squared up and punched the warden hard in the chest. From where I was standing it looked like he landed a solid blow. The warden doubled over and coughed. "You better not let anyone else die in here!" Nick screamed.

We expected the guards to retaliate, but they didn't make a move. They knew they were in a jam. 4 guards against 300 or 400 angry prisoners? They knew they were up against it and they backed down. Nick never got put in the hole for what he did, which they might have seen as a trade for what they had done to Herman. I don't know. There's not a lot of sense to be made out of life in prison.

One day John and I were sitting in the prison yard and I asked if he knew of anyone in Lansing that was actually innocent. That he knew for sure was innocent. And he pointed out a guy named Jack. Jack wasn't the only person who claimed to not have committed the sin that put him in prison, but he was the only one who John actually believed.

Jack had been sent to prison a few years earlier on a burglary charge. About a year into his sentence he tried to escape on the back of a trash truck, but he got caught before he even made it outside the walls. That cost him another few years of his freedom. Then, while he's sitting in prison serving time for the burglary and the attempted breakout, another guy gets sent to Lansing for the same burglary that Jack was convicted for committing. Somehow they convicted two guys for the same crime without even realizing it! More meat for the grinder I guess. Eventually justice prevailed and they found Jack innocent of the burglary he'd never committed, but he was still stuck in prison serving the time from his escape attempt. An escape he never would've had to attempt if he hadn't been wrongfully convicted in the first place. Like I said, sometimes prison has a sick sense of humor.

In prison, there was a standard uniform, and you could tell where a guy worked by the clothes he was issued. If you wore jeans and a pinstriped shirt, you worked in the Tag Factory. If you wore jeans and a white shirt, you worked in the main dining room or kitchen.

And if you wore white jeans with a white shirt, that meant you worked in the Officer's Mess. Some of the guards who wanted to save up a little money actually lived inside the prison walls. They slept in the prison dormitory, hung out in the staff rec room, and ate in the Officer's Mess.

One day John and I were coming back from the Tag Factory when we spotted our buddy Joe by the Officer's Mess. He's got on white pants with a white shirt. Joe was doing 10-21 for robbery. (He eventually did 11 years and got out.) I turned to John and said, "They couldn't be that stupid, right?!"

It seems to me that one of the unwritten rules of life is that you never want to piss off the person who's cooking your food. And there's not too many people more pissed off than prisoners. We asked Joe about it and sure enough, they had him working the Officer's Mess and he was giving a new definition to the word "mess". Joe hated cops with a passion and he was doing everything he could to make them regret eating within the prison walls. For months he had been adding ground up bugs and glass and all manner of unspeakable bodily fluids into the food that was being served to the prison's senior staff. A week after we learned this, they shut down the Officer's Mess forever.

Joe a good guy and was tight with another friend of ours named Pat who had been a tattoo artist on the outside. Joe was in for robbery. Pat had been caught stealing a watermelon out of a freezer and they gave him 5-10 years. It would have been a simple theft charge, but the freezer had a lock on it. He busted the lock, so it became a burglary charge. 5-10 years of his life for stealing a watermelon?!

A couple years later, Joe and Pat would be charged with killing a guy named Don. I never liked Don; he thought he was tough, and he acted like a bully. There were a lot of tough guys at Lansing, but they only acted tough when they needed to. Not that it justified them killing him, but nobody really missed him after he was gone.

Joe was found not guilty of Don's murder. Pat plead out to 10 to 20 years concurrent years, which included his previous 5 to 10 year charge. One day when I was talking to Pat after he was charged, I was joking around and I told him, "You got 5-10 for one watermelon. Seems like Don's life was only worth about two watermelons." I thought it was pretty funny, but Pat didn't feel much like laughing.

Getting Back at the Guards

I had been in prison about 6 months when I heard about a plan to get revenge on one of the guards, a guy named Adams. You could tell the rank of the guards by the color of the band on their hat. Black for a regular officer, silver for a lieutenant, and gold for the captains. There was a major too, but you never saw him unless you were really in trouble. I heard that Adams was writing guys up for dust on their bars and other petty stuff. He was a military-looking guy; a total asshole. If you got convicted for dust on your bars it was 30 days loss of good time; which changes your parole and discharge dates. The last thing you want to do is mess with the parole dates of a bunch of hardened criminals.

The streets that ran through Lansing Prison were made of bricks and were old enough that in certain areas, you could pull the bricks up from the road with your bare hands. The inmates of B Cell House, where Adams was an overseer, had been collecting bricks from the road. At 8am every morning the guards yelled, "Gang's Out" to release the inmates for work and on this morning, when they made the work call, a half-dozen guys started throwing the bricks down from the fifty feet above, trying to land a direct shot on Adams' head.

When I heard what happened, I went to B Cell House to check things out. It turned out that they didn't kill the guard, but he would never be right again. Some guys exaggerated the story, saying stuff like, "half of his brains were hanging out," but either way they messed him up. Everybody said he got what he deserved.

A month or so later in Cell House C, they hired another guard who started to do the same thing that Adams did, writing people up for dust on their bars. This guy thought he was the cock of the walk and wanted everyone to know it. Apparently, he didn't get the memo about what happened to Adams.

The inmates weren't dumb and knew that the best weapon they had on their side was gravity. This time instead of using bricks, they grabbed one of the tooling blocks that was used for tooling leather. These blocks were about 15 inches square, about 5 inches thick, and weighed around sixty pounds.

This guard, the cock of the walk, was sitting in his office cheap plywood office on the bottom floor of Cell House C. From the top tier of the cell block, it was a clear shot straight down to the ceiling of the office. It reminded me of a scene from a Wily Coyote cartoon where he tries to drop a safe on the Roadrunner.

One of the inmates held the block over the railing and dropped it over his target. By all accounts, it should have sliced right through the plywood and killed the guard below, but this was his lucky day. On the way down, the block was snagged by a wire that kept it from falling to the ground. It fell through the office ceiling but didn't touch the guard sitting inside.

When he looked up and had saw the tooling block hanging by a thread, the guard jumped up and ran out of the cell house; out of the prison. A few days later I went by the office to clown on the guard a little bit. I asked them, "where's that bad ass guard from C Block?". They told me he didn't even come back for his check.

After a while the guards learned who they could fuck with and who should be left alone, but sometimes they just couldn't help themselves. There was a convict at Lansing named Paul that turned out to be the wrong guy to fuck with. Before ending up in prison he'd lived in Leavenworth, Kansas, about 8 miles from the prison, so he knew some of the guards from growing up there. They knew him, but that didn't mean they liked him. One of the head guards,

Lieutenant Carter, had a daughter around Paul's age and they'd dated before his time at Lansing. Nobody knew exactly why, but Carter hated Paul with a passion and he and his goons took Paul to the hole and worked him over for the smallest breach of the rules.

Carter may have been a tough guy inside the prison, but when Paul got out a few months later, they were walking the same streets once again. A few weeks after he got out, we read in the paper that Lieutenant Carter had been beaten with a baseball bat as he was coming out of a bar in Leavenworth. Broke a few bones and sent him to the hospital for a while. Everybody in the joint knew who did it, but nobody ever got caught.

Everyone at Lansing was a convicted felon, but that didn't mean we were all the same kind of criminals. There were guys like Paul who were in and out in a year and then there were some real hard cases. Guys who knew they would spend the rest of their lives inside the system. One of the guys in Lansing at that time was Idabel Johnson. He was called Idabel because he was from Idabel, Oklahoma, and he and his partner-in-crime had killed a couple people while committing a robbery in Kansas City. The partner fled to Missouri where he was caught and eventually executed. Idabel escaped to Kansas where he killed a farmer, got a life sentence, and then he was sent to Lansing.

Even by prison standards, Idabel was a cold-hearted killer. After he got to Lansing he killed seven more people on the yard. They sent him to the hole, but that didn't stop him. Somehow, when he was in solitary confinement, he still managed to kill another inmate with a ball point pen. After that, they put him there as 'Permanent Party.' Now, in addition to being in prison for life, he would serve every second of his life sentence in the hole.

I respected Idabel because he had nerve, maybe a little too much nerve at times. He was about my size – around 6 feet tall - and had blond hair and bright blue eyes. I met Idabel the first time I was sent to the hole. As it turned out, I was sent to the hole a lot for breaking the rules and talking back to the guards, so Idabel Johnson and I ended up seeing quite a bit of each other.

Everything was tightly controlled in solitary, but that didn't mean that we couldn't smuggle things in and out. Somewhere along the line, an inmate had discovered that the handles in the food service carts were hollow and easy to fill with drugs, money or other small contraband. That made it easy to slip some illegal goods into the bean hole along with a guy's lunch.

Ironically, the whole smuggling operation was almost brought down by a missing spoon. Prison guards working the hole were required to have an inventory of everything that went in and came out of the cells (that they knew of!), and one day a metal spoon came up missing. None of the prisoners admitted having it and the guards were about to shake down each of the cells until the head guard called them off. No one was happy about it, especially Idabel, and we all wanted to know who had the spoon just as much as the guards.

A few days after I was released back into the general population, I saw a guy named Jessie Bolan showing off the spoon, bragging about how he got away with taking it. I knew Bolan was a tough guy (I found out later that he had been a professional boxer before ending up behind bars), but I was pissed that he almost got us busted over some bullshit. I walked up to him that day and threw my hardest punch.

There were only two punches thrown in that fight. My punch barely moved him and Bolan's first punch broke my nose, and I dropped like a bag of rocks right in front of Tower 13. Which was the worst place to get into a fight since you had no chance of getting away with it.

I staggered into A Cell House, trying to stop the blood as it seeped in between my fingers and knowing this wasn't a garden-variety bloody nose. A few days later, I had an operation to repair the damage to my face. That guy could really punch! After I got out of the hospital, I was sent to the hole for the fight. Talk about adding insult to injury.

John and I told Idabel what had happened with the spoon and the fight with Jesse Bolan and he got real quiet. Angry quiet.

Just because Idabel lived in the hole didn't mean that he lacked connections throughout the prison. After hearing what happened, Idabel sent word to his partners to take care of Bolan. They got to him when he was sitting in the barber chair in A Cell, getting his hair cut. A couple guys held him in the chair while the rest of the crew stabbed him repeatedly with shanks and knives. Bolan was left with scars all over his body and face. He didn't die, but he never came back out to the yard again. In prison you have your prize fighters and your surprise fighters, and even the strongest guy doesn't have a chance against an attack he doesn't see coming.

First Riot

I had been at Lansing about 6 months when I experienced my first prison riot.

As prisoners, we didn't have many privileges, but one of the small freedoms given to us was that if you didn't want to eat the food from the main line in the chow hall, you could fix yourself something in the kitchen. So when a guard came into the kitchen while some inmates were making hamburgers, and threw the burgers in the trash, that was a major violation of the unwritten rules.

Throwing away the hamburgers wasn't the only cause of the riot, and it probably wasn't even the main cause, but it was the final indignity that allowed the dam to break. And when it broke, it carried the weight of all the indignities and injustices that had been inflicted upon the Lansing inmates for years. The riot started in the chow hall, but it quickly spread to every corner of the prison that the inmates could reach. The mob burnt down the tag factory, the sign and marker department, the cannery and the paint factory. The damage would end up costing millions of dollars to repair, and all over a dozen hamburgers.

I was in A&T at the time the riot jumped off. A&T stood for Adjustment and Treatment and was another name for solitary confinement or The Hole. I don't know about the adjustment, but you sure get your treatment. Inside of A&T there were two more cells locked behind a set of big green doors. Being locked behind the green doors was the highest level of custody at Lansing. It was our own Black Hole of Calcutta. Behind the green doors you were naked and lived without light for 23 hours a day.

From the regular A&T cells, outside of the green doors, we heard some commotion from the riot up in the yard and one guy yelled out, "What's going on?"

The guard yelled back, "Just sit tight, the warden's gonna' show you what's going on real quick."

About 5 minutes later, I heard a roar and I looked out the bean hole just in time to see the fog moving in. Then I smelled it. Pepper gas. Five minutes later, you couldn't see a foot in front of you; if you could even open your eyes. At first, guys were putting their heads over the toilet, covering their heads with a blanket, and flushing the toilet. This would give us a couple breaths of fresh air, but then the guards found out what we were doing and turned off the water. So there was no air moving, no water flowing, nothing – just a stagnant cloud of gas. This is what they call "Mass Treatment". Even after a few days, the gas has stuck to everything. If you shook your blanket too hard getting into bed you would get gassed again.

When I got out of the hole later that week, the riot was still going on! I went back C block and got the scoop from John, Joe, and a guy named Kenny Hall. They told me that some of the prisoners were cutting their own Achilles tendons as a form of protest. They knew the prison would have to take care of them and it would be really expensive for them to treat, so they were disabling themselves willingly. While they were catching me up on the developments, a guard came into the building, shot the ceiling a few times with his rifle, and yelled at us, "Lock down and to find a cell!"

We jumped in the first cell on the bottom tier. It just so happened that it was the same cell that Tar got burned up in. The cell was still gutted and would need a new toilet and bunk before anyone could move in. While we waited in the burned-out cell, Joe took the opportunity to count his duckets. That's how prison was: exciting for a second and then you're bored again, even during a riot. Duckets were basically prison money that you could use to make purchases at the canteen, which was the prison store. Duckets came in 1s, 5s, and 10s. I asked Joe how much money he had, and he said he had about $22 or so. Then he said, "I got more money here than the guy I robbed coming out of a movie theater." Joe ended up doing 11 years for that robbery.

Only two guys got hurt during the riot. It happened when they robbed the canteen. A guy named Horse got shot stealing a bunch of leather goods and a guy named Lynch got killed. No one was too surprised, since Lynch seemed like he wanted to get out of prison, dead or alive. He and another guy were in for armed robbery, and they got loaded up with time. Lynch loved to gamble, but wasn't very good at poker, and he went on a losing streak playing cards in the yard until he ran out of money. But that didn't stop him. Lynch got credit from Butch, who ran the poker game, and quickly lost that money as well. He didn't care if he lost – he didn't really care about anything. He was playing with fire and it wasn't going to be long before it took his life. I felt bad for Lynch and I gave him five cartons of cigarettes to pay off his debt to Butch. I made him promise never to gamble again and as far as I know he never did until the day he died during the riot.

The riot eventually ended after the national guard was called in to help put it down. The main concession made to the prisoners was offering every inmate parole eligibility after 15 years, no matter the crime or the sentence. The most memorable parole hearing was Smoothie's. After what he'd done trying to escape with Tar, he wasn't ever getting out of prison, and everyone knew it. Smoothie went in front of the parole board and foreman of the board said, "I'll tell you what, the minute we see Officer Kanege walk through that door, you'll be a free man." Needless to say that murdered guard never walked through the door, and Smoothie never breathed air outside the prison walls.

One of the casualties of the riot was Warden Wilson, who was removed from his post soon after and replaced by Warden Gaffney. Gaffney weighed about 300lbs and rode a little Honda scooter around the prison yard, which, in addition to exaggerating his weight, made him look like an idiot. He's supposed to be the most powerful man at the penitentiary and here he's going around looking like some European tourist.

About 6 months later, I was reading the local newspaper and came across an article about cattle that were coming up missing on the prison ranch. It might seem odd today, but most of the larger prisons were self-sufficient back then. They had farms outside of the walls, along with herds of cattle, pigs, and other animals to keep the inmates fed. When asked him about it, Gaffney said that "wild dogs got them."

Someone must've found out the truth, because the new Warden wasn't around much longer after that. They found out he was running his own personal cattle business on the side. After that, I didn't really pay attention to who was chosen to be the next warden. Probably another crooked politician or cop, I figured. I didn't give a fuck. They were all crooked. One warden gets a guy killed through his own negligence, and the other is selling off cattle to line his pockets. These guys are supposed to be shining examples of morality and they're committing crimes that are worse than what a lot of guys at Lansing had done.

In the process of rebuilding the prison after the riot, they added a plasma donation center and a recreation center, which I helped to build. I worked on the big saw that cut the cinder blocks. That was a lot of trust to let an inmate use machinery like that, and as they say, no good deed goes unpunished. We found that the big saw was very good for making knives that we called shanks, or dirks. They weren't much to look at, but they would do the job. It gave me some prison status, since I only made them for my friends or guys who wanted to trade a favor.

Not long after the riot, I was sitting in the cell, just thinking. I was friends with Nick the Greek, who ran the poker table. John and I ran a store selling contraband items inside the prison. And Edgar was one of the toughest guys in the joint. He was nicknamed Baby Bull. During the riot, he had pulled iron bars out of the wall so the inmates could get into the canteen. He was comic book superhero strong. So altogether, we controlled the poker game and the store and had our own muscle for protection. I was quite pleased with my position in the prison after less than a year inside.

As a sideline to our business in selling contraband, we also had a hand in pretty much any alcohol production at the prison. We had the sugar, the yeast, and even the still. Larry Bland was a guy I had met in jail and then we were reunited at Lansing when he was sent to prison for forgery. His game on the streets was being a printer. Printing up forged checks, which was pretty much the same as printing money. He was real good at it, but then he slipped up and got busted - 15 years flat. He got a job at the prison's soap factory, and over time he acquired enough spare parts to build a still. After that there was a fairly steady supply of prison hooch coming off the still. My job was distribution. I would pack the alcohol across the yard and get a third of the booze as my cut.

There were a handful of guys brewing up booze at Lansing, but not everybody was doing it as well as Larry. Calling it "Toilet Wine" wasn't just a joke, guys were actually drinking their liquor out of the toilet. When the brewing process didn't go as planned, some guys might add something extra to give some kick to their beverage. There was a guy called Snooze who poured some typewriter ink into his batch of hootch to try to make up for a lack of alcohol and ended up killing a guy, blinding two others, and half-blinding himself.

In one of the all-time stupid job assignments by a prison, Larry was given a job working in the print shop! Of course, it wasn't long before he was printing up counterfeit duckets. The duckets were punch cards with spots for quarters, dimes and nickles adding up to the total amount. When you spent money from a ducket, the guy working the canteen would punch out the correct amount and hand you back the card. The only thing you had to do with the counterfeit duckets, was not spend all of the money on the card. The scheme ran well for awhile until a guy called Sid the Jew forgot the rule and let one of the fake duckets get through. It was swell while it lasted, but that was it for that scheme.

I didn't smoke cigarettes, but they were maybe the most common form of currency in prison. Even more common than actual money. My drugs of choice were opioids and I would trade cigarettes for pharmaceuticals like Darvon and Talwin. One thing I learned in prison was how to get the buffer out of the pharmaceutical pills so you could shoot them up. I also learned how to enhance the high by adding epson salt to the drugs.

My other addiction in prison was reading. I could read 5 or 6 books a day on a good day. And it wasn't just dime-store novels either. I got my hands on stuff like the Physicians Desk Reference and of course there was a copy of the Anarchist Cookbook floating around. That book taught me how to make a gun that would kill no matter where the bullet hits someone. I never had a chance to try it out, but it sounded quite Interesting.

From time to time, the prison would be visited by a celebrity or a musician and it was a big deal for the inmates. Mr. Folsom Prison Blues himself, Johnny Cash, came through Lansing while I was there. Unfortunately, I was in the hole at the time, so I only got to hear the stories from other guys.

Another time, the prison brought in a weightlifter named Paul Anderson for an exhibition. In the 60s, he was known as one of the strongest men in the world. He was one of the guys who would pull buses and airplanes by himself. He was a religious person; he talked soft and was really friendly to the inmates.

He put on an exhibition in the prison auditorium. At one point of the show he took out a metal spike about 10 inches long and a piece of wood that was about 5 ft long and 6 inches thick. He secured the board between two tables, took out a hammer, and pounded the spike into the board about 1 inch or so.

Then he pulled out a silk handkerchief and, like a magician, turned it over to show everyone that it was just a hanky. He wrapped the thin cloth around his hand and squeezed his fingers into a tight fist. Before we even realized what was happening, Anderson lifted the fist over his head and brought it down with such force that it drove the spike through the wood and out the other side.

We were speechless. I thought of myself as a strong, tough guy, but this was another kind of strength. I don't think I could've driven that spike in one swing with a sledgehammer, and he did it with his fist and a hanky. He may not be as famous as Johnny Cash, but he sure put on a heck of a show.

I might not have been able to drive that spike with a hammer, but there were a few guys who probably would've loved to have an arm-wrestling match with Paul Anderson. One of the prison's strongest guys just happened to be serving with his two brothers. It's wasn't uncommon to meet two siblings serving in prison together, but to have Robert, Isaiah, and Grantville Jackson serving together at Lansing was a bit of an oddity.

They were all athletes, and Robert was the strong one. Guys said he held some records for weightlifting in his weight class, which was around 165 lbs. He could bench 425lbs, squat 500, and deadlift 600. He was also a really nice person, so he didn't end up using his strength for violence.

Robert's brother Isaiah was a baseball player. They called him Fireball Jackson because of his blistering fastball, but he could hit a bit as well. In one of the games played between inmates, I saw him hit a ball over the Center Field Tower. It was 396 feet to center, with another 25 vertical feet of wall, fence and barbed wire to clear. That was the hardest hit baseball I ever saw on that field. (There was a door at the base of the tower the led to the gallows.

Before ending up in Lansing, Isaiah's baseball skills had gotten him a tryout for the Pittsburgh Pirates. He wanted to be a pitcher, but they didn't like his prospects in the major leagues, because could only throw a fastball. The Pirates thought his arm might be an asset in the field and suggested that he try the outfield, where he was an instant success. He could throw a ball from deep center to home plate on a line. No need for a cut-off man. It looked like Isaiah was on his way to a professional baseball contract until he got caught robbing a cab driver. Turns out he was still on parole from a previous conviction and his petty thievery of the cab driver landed him back at Lansing. At least he had family there I guess.

Isaiah wasn't the only guy at Lansing who almost made it as a professional athlete. There was an inmate we called Jump-Jump Jones who had been a basketball star in his hometown. This man was talented. He could jump flat-footed from under the basketball hoop, put his arm through the rim, and hang there by his elbow. He was a good man who did a bad thing. But I guess that's how a lot of us would've described ourselves. Jump-Jump had been recruited out of high school to play at one of the big basketball colleges and to sweeten the deal, they gave him a new car and some spending money. He was even featured in Sports Illustrated in an article about inmates with exceptional athletic talent. Apparently, they didn't give him enough money, because shortly after receiving the car, he robbed a convenience store and killed the two elderly store owners in the process. A cop tried to pull him over as he fled the scene, but Jump-Jump hit the gas and tried to escape. He ended up losing control of the car, veering off the side of the road into a lake.

The cop who had been chasing him dove in and pulled him out of the water. Jump-Jump Jones was bleeding pretty badly from the crash and coincidentally, a nurse returning from work happened to drive by at that very moment and stopped to help save his life.

It was a mixed blessing. Jump-Jump survived the accident, but he would spend the rest of his life behind bars.

Race Riot

The next year there was another riot at Lansing, but this riot was different than the one in '68. This wasn't a rebellion against the prison guards, this was a race riot. This was a couple years before the big riot in Attica, but there were already riots going on in prisons all over the country. In early 1969, prison officials decided to bring a group of young inmates up from the reformatory in Hutchinson, Kansas. They were sent to Lansing after there had been fighting between the gangs of blacks and whites in Hutchinson. The worst offenders from these two groups were pulled out and sent to Lansing. One black group and one white group. I don't know who thought this would settle things down, but it just spread the disease to a new host.

A few days before the riot started, John asked me to go to Robert Jackson and see if he wanted "the fixings." The fixings is what we called the raw materials for making booze. Ten pounds of sugar, a pack of yeast, and a gallon of tomato puree were the basics of making prison home brew or pruno. Robert lived on 10 walk, which was the top level of the cell block, probably 60 feet above the ground. Robert and his brothers were some of the head honchos in the black community at Lansing and even the new guys had to respect them. As I reached the top of the stairs on 10 walk, I ran into a group of black guys, most of them recently arrived from Hutchinson. I could see they wanted to throw me off of the tier; they hated whites. But I just walked right past them to Robert's cell. They knew who I was and who I was going to see and they weren't stupid enough to make enemies of their own race. Robert paid me for the fixings: 10 packs of cigarettes for the sugar, 5 packs for yeast and 2 packs for the tomato puree. It was one of the last normal days we would have at Lansing for a while.

The shit hit the fan in the recreation building a couple of days later. Nothing too fancy, just gangs of white and black prisoners doing battle with fists and shanks and anything else they could fashion into a weapon. A guard stationed in the tower behind C Cell house had seen what was going down and started shooting to keep the fight from spilling out into the yard. Only guy got across under fire, a black guy named Gene. I had hung out with him before the riot and got along with him well. I ran up to him and said, "You know this isn't right?" He just shrugged.

After the fight in the rec building, the guards pretty much decided to let these groups handle the situation by themselves. They were outnumbered 70 to 1 in there, so if inmates wanted to fight, they would find a way. The next day, shit started going down in the Chow Hall. A white guy named George, who was in for multiple murders, pulls out a gun and starts shooting into a crowd of black guys. Who knows how he got the gun, but the riot was back on. The blacks had done more damage in the clash in the Rec Building, but the Whites got revenge against them in the Chow Hall. Things returned back to normal after awhile, but during the riot it was goddam mess. Race Riots are really stupid as far as I am concerned. It's just prisoners fighting prisoners, and in the end no one wins. If you're going to put your life on the line, at least do it fighting against your oppressors.

After the riot, they reversed course and sent all of the young guys back to Hutchinson. Just a colossal fuckup, but I'd wager good money that no one lost their job over it.

Life was just starting to get back to normal after the riot when I was called into see my case manager and informed that I would be transferred to Hutchinson. I protested, but they didn't want to hear it. They were going to send me and the decision was final. I asked if they were going to change my sentence, which sometimes happened when you got transferred, but they said that wasn't part of the deal. I did receive parole eligibility a year and a half earlier than I would have gotten it otherwise, but that was certainly no guarantee that I'd be getting out any sooner.

So I went to Hutchinson. I was there for 3 weeks: one week in the fish tank, one week in population, and one week in the hole. Before

I went into the general population, they asked where I wanted to work. I told them I wanted to work in the gym with a guy called Coach Love, because I had heard what he had done for another guy named Paul "Boogie" Stovall. Boogie ended up playing professional basketball after he got out and it was mostly due to Coach Love teaching him how to play basketball while he was at Hutchinson. I was assigned to work with Coach Love; an assignment that only lasted one week.

After my first week in the general population, more shit between the whites and the blacks kicked off in the cell house. Guys were picking up the heaviest things they could, which were the chairs, and throwing them across the room at each other. Eventually, after things calmed down, we were all taken to this big area they called the rotunda. All the inmates were there, and the guards asked people to speak their piece about how to deal with the riots. No one would say anything at first, but eventually I spoke up. I told them this place is "the shits" because the food was so bad compared to Lansing. They also seemed content to live in their own filth. In the chow hall there were plastic pitchers on the tables for your drinks. Prisoners would take their leftover food after their meal and throw it in those pitchers. Just leaving a nasty soup of food scraps and iced tea. I told them that it was disgusting, and they should have some respect for themselves, but I don't think it made much of an impression on them.

Reformatory life was a little different than life at the prison. For one thing, if you got on someone's bad side, they wouldn't kill you, but they had other ways of making you suffer. The other inmates would sneak up on you and cut off a chunk of your hair. Or cut off a pant leg. It was called giving a guy 'a panic' and putting someone on a panic was a way of testing their mentality. It was a warning. The inmates at the top of the prison food chain were saying, "You are not wanted here." If you saw someone who'd been put on a panic, you knew that person was basically a rat. In Lansing they'd have been dead.

My outspoken, negative attitude toward incarceration was not appreciated at Hutchinson, and after 3 weeks I was back at Lansing. They didn't appreciate the things I had to say about their facility, so they sent me back. That was just fine with me, since Lansing still felt like home. It was a pretty dogshit place to call home, but it was all I had at the time.

When I went back to Lansing, I pretty much picked up where I'd left off. Kidwell, the State Legislator was still living in his mobile home next to the Warden's house. He probably heard some of the commotion during the riots, but he never felt the fear that the other prisoners felt. Every time I caught a glimpse of his mobile home through a prison window, my blood boiled. It was a complete injustice and it was right there on display for anyone to see. As long as we have different strokes for different folks, we won't ever have justice in this country.

After the race riot, things got back to normal. I'd been the new guy at Hutchinson, so it was nice to be back among friends at Lansing. One day on the yard, John and Nick introduced me to a guy named Duck. I don't know why they called him that, his thing was dice. After I got to know him a little bit, he was willing to show me the trade secrets of how to cheat at dice. I never used this knowledge to cheat, but I learned how to keep the cheat off of me. You hear a guy cheating because the sound is different. As you might imagine, cheating was pretty common in prison, and the consequences for getting caught were usually serious.

One day I was handing out socks in the cell house and Joe was in there practicing his "cheating skills." He asked me if I could see him dealing seconds (he could slide the top card back to see it and then deal off the bottom if he wants it). I couldn't see anything off about his dealing, but even in cards, you will hear a man cheating more than see him. Joe was one of the top dogs at Lansing, but that didn't mean he wouldn't cheat at poker. Setting up a poker game on the yard was a year-round event. In the dead of winter, prisoners would shovel a clearing in the snow to make a space to play poker outside.

Joe found himself in one of these winter poker games in the winter of 1969 - everyone huddled around wearing heavy coats and blowing into their hands to keep warm. It might sound crazy to play outside in the winter, but there was barely any heat inside the cell block – just 6 little radiators for more than 100 cells – so it didn't really matter if you were inside or outside, you we're going to freeze either way.

Poker was serious business in the pen. Nick "The Greek" ran one game and Shakey Reese ran the other one. One time I ran into Shakey Reese in his cell before his poker game and he was rolling up magazines and taping them around his torso. Then he wrapped himself in a blanket and wore a big jacket over the top. He told me it was protection in case someone tried to stab him during an argument over the game.

At Lansing, we played poker with a stripped deck. We would take out all of the kings and put in two jokers, so 50 cards total. We played normal poker hands, but aces were always low and jokers could be used with anything. There were two types of decks you could get at the canteen: one had a red design on the back and the other one was blue. So Joe was playing this poker game in the middle of winter and he had a straight in either pocket – blue-backed cards on one side and red-backed cards on the other side. Joe waited for a big pot and when it was time to show his dog of a hand, he switched the cards with the winning hand in his pocket. Only it wasn't the same color of the deck they were using. Joe was caught dead-to-rights, and almost everybody at the table had killed men and most would've done it again, but Joe just leaned back and said, "Fuck all you guys!" Anyone but Joe, they would have killed him, but Joe was damn near untouchable, and he knew it.

One of the most valuable things you could learn in prison was who was connected and who had each others' backs. Some guys thought you could get respect by beating up another guy or even killing him, but that didn't mean shit if you didn't have any friends.

It just put a target on you. A young guy by the name of Terry Strobel came into the joint and within less than a month was killed by a guy called T-Bird who wanted to make a reputation for himself. Not long after, T-Bird and I got into it at the Rec Shack. They didn't have a regular sized pool table, but they a bumper pool table and T-Bird and I were playing a game when I hit a ridiculous trick shot. I was just messing around and hit a massé shot that curved around a bumper and went right in the hole. The guys who were watching couldn't believe it either and they started laughing like crazy. T-Bird thought they were laughing at him and he didn't like that, so he came at me. I slashed at him with the tip of the pool cue and left a cut on his cheek. He staggered back and I turned the pool cue around to the big end and swung it in his direction. He regained his confidence for a moment, but then lost his nerve just as fast. He knew if he didn't stop, he was about to really get hurt. More than that cut on his cheek, and more than the damage I was going to do with the fat end of the stick. He knew that if he started shit with me, he was starting shit with my whole crew. And most guys at Lansing would rather French kiss a rattle snake then fuck with us. T-Bird backed down that day and never stepped up to me again. I guess he had found his place on the prison food chain.

Parole Board

I saw a parole board for the first time in 1971. When I went in front of the board, I had a good parole plan. I was going to go to work for AAA Insurance in Topeka and I would be getting paid good money to haul cars for them all over Kansas. It was going to be my chance to finally put my knowledge of cars to use for good and maybe have a chance at a normal life.

But it didn't work out that way. I ended up getting a year set off, which means I got one year off of my sentence, but I was denied parole. After the set off, I still had a year and six months left on my sentence, without a chance to see the parole board for another year.

If that wasn't bad enough, at the same time I had my parole denied, Thomas Kidwell, the wife-killing state legislator, got paroled. When he went in front of the parole board, he got his first parole for murder, and I got denied mine for theft and a parole violation. The day I heard about Kidwell, I was already mad as hell about my own situation and I ran over to D cell house to get a look over the prison wall. Sure enough, the mobile home was gone. Most people who get paroled have to wait 30 to 60 days for what we called kick outs – when they finally got to leave. Kidwell was gone within 24 hours of seeing the board. This guy got preferential treatment from the day he arrived at Lansing until the day he left.

For me, that was kind of the straw that broke the camel's back. Whatever part of me had wanted to stay on the straight and narrow before was gone, and all I had left was pure hatred for the system and the people who were in control of it.

After getting my parole denied, I didn't give much of a fuck about anything. I still had good money coming in: Nick still had the poker game going, John and I ran the store, and I had 1/3 interest in a still. But that wasn't enough. I was losing my mind in there and I just wanted to get back at the prison system.

So I robbed the canteen. Not 1 time, but 5 times. Fuck Them!!!! Not only did I rob the store, but I also robbed the prison librarian. I didn't care if he was a librarian or not, he worked for the prison and so he was on their side. It wasn't exactly the perfect crime: John and I put pillow cases over our heads and threatened the guy with homemade knives until he turned over his watch and ring. What we didn't know at the time was that he was a Kansas Bureau of Investigations Agent in disguise.

They never had any hard evidence against us, and the KBI agent couldn't identify us, but we still ended up in the hole. They knew it was us and in prison there's no innocent until proven guilty. They could have taken us over to the Leavenworth County Courthouse to give us a formal hearing, but instead they just took away our good time. It was as good as another sentence because it was costing us more years of our lives. At that point I had accumulated 4 ½ years of good time, which they took away at our disciplinary hearing. The disciplinary hearings were a total sham; a classic kangaroo court.

After looking over the evidence in Kangaroo Court, the Major would pronounce you guilty or not guilty. I couldn't help but laugh because the whole thing was so obviously rigged. After the major pronounced my guilt for robbing the KBI agent, I said, "When you walk through the doors, you already decided to find us guilty, whether we did it or not!" Then I told him where he could stick his write ups. That got him really pissed off and I could see he wanted to hit me, but instead he yelled, "El Rod!!! El Rod!" That was the nickname of one of the guards, a black lieutenant that would escort you to the hole.

After the hearing we were still in the hole without any notion of when we might be let out. They'd taken our good time, but that wasn't enough. After a couple weeks in the hole, John asked the head guard if, hypothetically, he knew the location of the ring and the watch, would they let us out of the hole? A couple days later we were back in general population after the ring and watch were miraculously found. Who knows if they even got back to the KBI agent or if the guards just pocketed them and never mentioned they were found.

Another year goes by and I get my shot in front of the parole board again. By that time, I'd served 4 years on my 5-10, but unlike my las time in front of the board, this time I wasn't expecting to get paroled. My plan for this hearing was to tell them that they could stick their Justice and their Order straight up their "mother fucking, cock sucking asses." In those exact words. I called them everything I could think of and cursed them until I was red in the face. "I will do this sentence day for day before I take a parole from you bunch of no good mother fucking bitches!" I screamed. By this point, I had no good time. According to the letter of the law, I would have to serve every day of my ten-year sentence.

Word got around about my parole hearing and pretty soon everybody in the joint knew what I had done. The prisoners either thought I was brave or stupid and the guards wouldn't talk to me at all. The only time the guards talked to me was to threaten to write me up. "I'll go get you the pen for you motherfucker!!" was my usual response.

I started on my 5th year in Lansing. My case manager was a guy by the name of Duckweiler; not a bad guy, just another cog in the machine. I was called to his office one day and he told me if I stayed out of trouble for two years, they would give me back all of my good time and I'd be free to go. He didn't understand that I was done making compromises. At that point, I would have stayed in Lansing for the rest of my life before I make any deals with the authorities.

My attitude and my connections meant that I was a constant irritant to everyone in charge at the prison. I kept getting write ups and getting myself sent to the hole, but I wore each punishment like a badge of honor. After a while, Duckweiler sends for me again and says if I stay out of trouble for one year, they would let me out and give me all of my good time back. I didn't give it a second's thought. Hell, I didn't give a shit if the sun rose or set and I damn sure didn't care about going to the hole again.

I had served almost five years on my sentence and Duckweiler pulls me in to meet again. This time, he tells me if I stay out of trouble for six months, he would give me all of my time back. No deal. I got more write ups. Then he tells me if I stay out of trouble for 90 days, they would sign my papers to let me out. I couldn't stay out of trouble for 90 days and they knew it! The hate I had for the system at that point couldn't be extinguished by the tortures I had to endure. They beat me, gassed me, and even took a fire hose to me when I was in A&T. It takes a sadistic person to turn a firehose on a man in a prison cell.

The charade went on and the next time we met, Duckweiler told me that if I could stay out of trouble for 60 days they will let me out and I could go home. Then a few weeks later Duckweiler drops it down to 30 days. Everybody in the joint knew I hated these pieces of shit and there wasn't any amount of time they could trade me for my servitude.

A couple weeks into this new deadline I got busted with 10 gallons of home brew in my cell and it looked like I was going back in the hole. I lived in a four-man cell and one of my cellmates was a guy named Lucas who was serving a life sentence at Lansing. He took the fall for me and told them it was his homebrew. The guards weren't stupid and they knew it belonged to me, but after he took the blame, they couldn't do anything to punish me. Two weeks later, I got out.

On my last day at Lansing I went to Receiving and Discharge to get dressed out and they gave me a suit that looked like it was made in the 30s and $107.65 in cash. Working in the prison, I had earned 10 cents a day - half to spend while I was locked up and half for my discharge. Every nickel of $107.65 is how long I was in.

When I told people about my time at Lansing, most of them didn't care or they didn't believe me. That's one of the reasons I'm writing this book. Millions of people are locked up in America every day just like I was, and in the eyes of society they are less than human.

We were as men who through a fen
Of filthy darkness grope;
We did not dare a breathe a prayer
Or give our anguish scope;
Something was dead in each of us,
And what was dead was hope.
- From 'The Ballad of Reading Gaol' by Oscar Wilde

I got out of Lansing in June of 1973, and the first thing I did was get a bus ticket back to Denver. I wanted to see my mother. She was still married to Clifford and, in contrast to the old saying, absence had NOT made the hear grow fonder. I still hated his guts, and he didn't feel much better toward me. But I loved my mother and it was good to see her again after so many years apart.

While I was in prison my sister Kathy had married a guy named Larry who I'd known since the first grade. When I got back to Denver they let me move in with them until I got my feet under me. Larry got me a job making campers in Commerce City and my first week on the job I made $107.63. That number felt like a sick joke. I made 107.65 cents for 5 and half years of work in Lansing and two cents more than that in one week of work on the outside.

That's when I met Vicki. She was a friend of Kathy's and once we starting seeing each other, things moved pretty quickly. We moved in together about a month after we met, and we were married within the year.

Now that I had a decent job and a woman in my life, you might think that I moved on from my life of crime, but I was still harboring so much anger from my time in Lansing and I felt I could get back at the system by doing whatever I wanted, regardless of what the law said. I tried to make up for lost time, but the more I thought about the time I'd lost, the more I wanted to get back at the people who had taken my life away. Not only was I an angry young man, I didn't think I'd ever have to worry about growing old. I thought I'd be dead before the age of thirty so I didn't have much concern for the future.

This is when I started my profession as a "steal worker". And I was pretty good at it. Because of the things I picked up in Lansing, I was a much more seasoned criminal when I left prison than I was when I went in. I had learned how to do all kinds of things like evading security systems, setting a fire without leaving behind evidence of what caused it, and what we called till tapping. We would hang around a department store on a slow business day and when the salesperson left the register we'd open the drawer and quickly pocket some cash – the secret was that you didn't take all the money, you leave enough in the drawer that it isn't obvious. It turned out I was a much better student in prison than I ever was in school and I made good use of the education I'd received on the inside.

My new brother-in-law Larry was also accustomed to living on the wrong side of the law and didn't back down from anyone. When we were in high school, a guy called Chuck Blood and some other guys jumped Larry. They beat him up pretty good, but Larry wasn't about to just take the beating, so the next day he brings a baseball bat to school and beats the hell out of the main guy. The kid was in the hospital for a couple days and nobody messed with Larry anymore.

After high school Larry was drafted and sent over to Europe, where did a year in the service working on the Army motor pool before going AWOL. He was getting restless in the Army and he was fascinated by the culture he encountered when he left the base, so he cut bait and galivanted around Europe for a while just living as a tourist. But even in a foreign country, criminals always seem to find each other. Larry fell in with some mid-level drug dealers in Berlin and started selling weed and pills to street dealers. Things were going well until Larry set up a deal with a guy who turned out to an informant for the German police. When the moment came to do the bust, Larry got wise to the situation and took off running, firing a gun back at the cops. He didn't his any of the police, but one shot hit the informant in the leg. No less than he deserved for being a rat.

The police eventually caught up with Larry and since he was in Europe, he had to go in front of a tribunal of judges and got 10 years. But after spending a few years in Europe, Larry was savvy to how the system worked. He asked his lawyer to offer the judges 10 thousand dollars as restitution and it actually worked! They lowered his sentence down to 3 years.

The prison experience in Germany was about 180 degrees from what I experienced at Lansing. Larry got day passes to leave the prison and he would go into town and mingle with the locals. They bonded over their love of Rock n Roll, which was only just a few years old, and they would sing Beatles songs together in German and English. When he completed his sentence, he was taken by the US military back to a military base in Texas where he was held until he was honorably discharged. After all that, he somehow managed to still get an honorable discharge. After coming back to Denver, Larry reconnected with my sister, got married and that's about when I showed up fresh out of Lansing.

Larry had a decent job, but he was always a restless guy who was looking to make some quick money, even if it meant breaking a few laws. We started doing string robberies, which was another thing I'd learned about in prison. String robberies are a series of robberies that you pull off back-to-back — we'd rob 4 or 5 places right when they opened up in the morning. Our reasoning was that there weren't any customers there yet, so there wouldn't be any witnesses. And then we'd rob another 4 or 5 places in the evening, mostly convenience stores. They didn't really have convenience stores when I was a kid, but then in the 70s, stores like 7-11 and Circle-K started popping up on every corner. Our robbery scheme worked well back then, but you'd be crazy to do the same thing now because of all the surveillance cameras.

When you're committing 10 robberies a day, you run out of places to rob pretty quickly. We ended up going back to the same stores to rob them every few weeks. One time we were entering a store and before I even made it to the counter the employee was already getting the money out of the register. I only had to get my gun out a few times and I never planned on using it.

It was around this time that I met one of Larry's army buddies named Tom Leask. We only met briefly and I didn't think much of him at the time, but his name was in the news a couple decades later for going on a rampage with heavy machinery in his hometown of Alma, Colorado.

Larry had rules about robbery: no bars, no liquor stores. These were more likely to be mom and pop businesses and a couple robberies could put them out of business. And they were a lot more likely to have guns. We'd ride around during the evening and discuss the robberies we wanted to commit the next day, scouting out each location. At our peak, we were robbing around 50 places a week. I think in the back of my mind I was kind of hoping that the cops would drive up on us so that I could take a shot at them. I was so pissed off at the system I didn't give a fuck what happened to me and every officer I saw in uniform was my enemy.

Committing string robberies was a pretty simple operation. One guy went into the store, one guy stayed in the car. I wore sunglasses and baseball cap and would go up to the counter and say, "This is a robbery, give me the money." Just like that, nothing fancy. I was usually out in less than a minute. Police response times weren't very good back then and we never ended up getting caught on the scene. Sometimes we'd listen for sirens to figure out which direction the cops were coming from and then drive off to rob another store in the opposite direction.

It's kind of amazing to me now that it took almost 6 months for us to get caught. We were out doing robberies one night and an off duty cop sees us parked in a car that they recognized from the robberies. They came to the apartment where we lived with a guy named Nick who was pulling out as the cops were headed to our apartment. They stopped Nick as he was leaving as Larry and I were escaping out of the back. The heat started to come down and so I decided to go into the wind. That's when I went to Wichita with Vicki. They filed an out of state warrant for the robberies in Colorado, but they didn't have any case against us, they just had a car tied to some robberies that was registered to my sister.

In Wichita I tried to keep my nose clean. I got a job. Lots of jobs actually and I went straight for quite a while. Vicki and I got married. She had a daughter named Robyn from a previous marriage and about a year after we were married we had a son we named Billy. I'll never forget the day, August 4th of 1974. These were actually the best years of my life. I was working for auto salvage businesses, and I bought a mobile home, which looked like the one the Kidwell lived in at Lansing.

Even though I was keeping it on the straight and narrow, I still had a lot of friends from my time in Lansing. Friends of mine would come over and we would use still use prison slang when we talked. We would use so much slang that my wife wouldn't know what we were talking about. The guys I didn't know from Lansing were in motorcycle gangs and were ex-convicts too, so we all spoke the same language.

Life was good at that point. Things weren't perfect and I still felt some of the anger I'd built up at Lansing, but it was getting better every year. Then, in July of 1975, I got arrested and charged for a murder I didn't commit.

The cops showed up at our trailer in the early evening and asked me to come down to the station to answer some questions. They didn't put cuffs on me and when I got to the station they took me to an interrogation room. I still didn't know why I was even there and I waited in the hot room for what seemed like forever.

Finally, a detective came in and started asking me questions about my whereabouts from a few days before. I felt like I didn't have anything to hide other than maybe some minor traffic violations, so I answered his questions. I couldn't tell what was happening – they hadn't read me my Miranda Rights but it felt like I was under arrest. I asked him if I was being charged for something and he screamed, "Yes!" That's when I knew I was mixed up in some serious shit. I clammed up and regretted saying anything to him.

After talking to the detective, I was charged with murder and booked into jail for a crime I didn't commit. In jail, I found out they had arrested another suspect in the murder who was identified by an eyewitness, which gave me a glimmer of hope, but my hope was short-lived. They dropped the charges on the other guy and charged me. All of this would eventually come out in court.

Some of the details of the case appeared in the Chanute Tribune on July 15th, 1975. The victim was Edwin "Bud" Helms, 38, resident of Sparta, Missouri, who was staying at the Oaks Kitchenette Motel in Wichita at the time of his death. He was set to start a new job at an aircraft plant on the day after his death.

The boy who witnessed the crime was staying in the room next to Helms and answered a knock at his door around 6pm from a man who asked to see Helms. Confused, the boy turned him away, and moments after closing the door on him, heard two gunshots ring out. It seems Helms had opened his door to investigate the activity next door and came face-to-face with his killer.

The newspaper story also includes the detail that Helms, apparently in fear for his life, has given a friend the name and address of a Kansas man and said if anything happened to him, to give the information to the police. The man was questioned by the police, but released.

When I was arrested for the murder, I didn't know what to think. Part of me thought it was just a misunderstanding that would be cleared up fairly quicky, but another other part of me felt like the system was about to swallow me up again. Each day I was in jail for a crime I didn't commit, my anger at the authorities returned.

Needless to say, it's a crazy feeling being on trial for a crime you didn't commit. Everyone else in court is acting deadly serious about their job and dotting every "i" and crossing every "t" and you're the only person who knows with 100% certainty that it's all a sham.

The detective took the stand at the trial and said that I had behaved like I was guilty in the interrogation because I hadn't answered all of his questions. They didn't have anything on me so they had to use behavioral psychology bullshit like that.

Then they put the eyewitness on the stand that had identified the first suspect. I found out he was only 16 at the time of the murder. He wasn't able to pick me out of a lineup, so the prosecutors tried to have him do a voice identification. They had me stand up and say, "Is Bud home?" and apparently that was good enough for the kid to know that I was the killer. It was a classic case of cops making the evidence fit their story.

There was also a black preacher who was staying in the room on the other side of Helms. The preacher took the stand and said that all he had seen was a silhouette or shadow that ran by his room, but he thought that the person he'd seen was bigger than me.

The trial wasn't without its humorous moments. The prosecution called a gun expert to that stand who said that the bullet that was found in Helms' body had to have come from a pistol instead of a rifle because of the slippage marks on the bullet. In cross-examination my lawyer asked the gun expert, "If a .32 rifle was used with the same caliber and had a loose bolt, it would cause the same slippage marks, right?" The gun expert said, "Yes." The judge caught the contradiction and interrupted the questioning, "You told everybody this bullet had to have come from a pistol." He told the Gun Expert to get off of the stand and tells him that he is not qualified to give expert testimony. I respected the judge for being impartial and not just taking the side of the police.

The trial wasn't just a sham because they didn't have any hard evidence against me, I also had multiple people who could testify to my whereabouts at the time of the murder. My lawyer had filled a Plea of Alibi at the start of the trial to prove that I was several miles away at the time of the murder. I had 6 witnesses that could testify that I was home! The married couple that lived to the east testified they had seen me at home at the time of the murder. A woman that lived to the west testified that she knew I was home at 6pm because she was on her way to a bingo game and had asked me if I wanted to go. Our neighbor across the street was leaving at the same time with her daughter and had seen us talking. The owner of the mobile home park had also seen me at home around that time.

The jury came back in less than 2 hours with a not guilty verdict. Just a waste of everyone's time and money. In the local newspaper it said "Motel Killer Free!" How the hell could I be the killer and be going free? I hated the police before, but at least I felt like I deserved some of the punishment I received. This time it was all for nothing. I now had a burning hatred for the cops as well as the District Attorney and the judges who'd put me in this position. I now understood that their attitude was to win at all costs. Even if it meant putting an innocent person behind bars. And if they can't convict you, they will do everything in their power to bankrupt you. They do not care as long as they can feel like they won.

Frustrated by the lack of a conviction in the murder trial, the DA was looking for any leverage against me and caught wind the case that has been filed against me for the string robberies in Colorado. When I was acquitted of the murder charge, the DA decide to refile that case on me. I never got out of jail after I was found not guilty – I was immediately extradited back to Colorado. A police officer took me the airport and when we got to the entrance of the terminal, I told the officer that he couldn't go inside. He asks me why not. I tell him, "Because it says right there, no animals allowed, you fucking pig!"

At the arraignment hearing, they called a police officer I'd never seen before to the stand. The string robberies had happened a few years before and apparently no one from the original case was available to testify. The officer said that he didn't know anything about the case except that another officer said he was involved, and that officer was basing his information off of something another officer had said. It was like a big game of telephone, but apparently the judge was convinced enough to hold me for a preliminary hearing. At the preliminary hearing, they had found a witness that I allegedly robbed. I thought they had me dead-to-rights, but when he got on the stand, the witness said that I wasn't the guy who had robbed him! The judge was pretty upset and he told him, "You picked him out of a line up and that's him right there, but now you are saying he didn't rob you!?" I don't know why he changed his mind – there's a good chance it was us who robbed him – but I wasn't about to ask any questions. After hearing his testimony, the judge dismissed the case.

I was finally set free again, but I had lost everything. I was broke. I had lost my home and my car and I was estranged from my wife and my kids. At this point, I didn't give a shit about anything anymore. I'd tried to live by the rules of polite society, but it just got me thrown back in jail. What was the point in following the rules if I was just labelled by the authorities as a criminal? So I got back together with Larry and went back into the steal business. Before long, I got arrested and went back to jail at the Adams County jail.

While I was in jail, my wife came to visit me with our son. We hadn't seen each other in more than a year and I missed them both terribly. We were given 10 minutes for a visit and we sat at a booth, divided by a glass barrier with a cutout like a little picture frame. We only had 10 minutes to talk and I was committed to making every second count. Just as we were starting to speak, about a minute into our conversation, a wooden barrier drops down between us, released by one of the guards. I was shocked and then quickly furious at the guard who had taken time with my family away from me. I guess he didn't like me and that was his way of letting me know it.

Well, I had way of letting the guards know I didn't like them either. The next morning, the same guard was on duty in the cellblock, picking up the empty breakfast trays. I rolled up a newspaper, lit it on fire and held the tray with a wet towel while my friend heated it up until it was red hot. I handed it out for the guard to pick it up and oh, you should have heard that piggy squeal like a little bitch. To me, he got what he deserved. I always try to follow the motto: "Don't get mad, get even!"

There's a code in jail that you don't ask a guy what he's in for, but some guys can't help giving you all the gruesome details. One day, a guy I was friendly with told me that there's a guy in our section of the jail bragging about raping his 7 and 11 year-old daughters. Absolutely vile shit. I wanted to check this out for myself so I sat down across from this guy at breakfast and ask him what he is in for. Like I said, most guys would be offended by this, but he was excited to tell me. He told me the details that I already knew and then told me that he broke his 11 year old daughter's arm with a bat because she was resisting him. He was bragging about it. He was talking like he was proud of what he did.

Word started to get around about him in our section of the jail and one day on the yard a group of guys jumped him and did as much damage as they could before the guards pulled him out and moved him to the next row of cells. It just so happened that Larry was in that section of the jail.

Larry came up to me the next day and asked me what was going on. I filled him in on all reasons why the rapist had been jumped and Larry promised that he'd get what was coming to him. After word got around and the guards were busy in another area, a group of guys tied the rapist to the bars of a cell. They gagged his mouth so he couldn't yell and they took turns beating and torturing the evil fuck! Larry stuck lit cigarettes up the guy's nose while they were beating the shit out of him. Scarred him up something good. They beat him for days until he was due in court, and then they dragged him to the front of the jail and dropped him in a heap. When the guards found him, they took him straight to the hospital.

They eventually charged Billy Campbell for the beating, but Billy had a lot of time already. He didn't give a damn about getting more time, so Billy was fine taking the charge. There's a certain kind of power a prisoner has when he knows he's never getting out.

When he went to court for the charge, the pedophiles wife, the mother of the two girls, was there. She came to thank Billy for beating the man who had raped her daughters. She wanted to be there to thank him for giving her some kind of justice, even if it wasn't justice under the law.

At this point in my life it felt like I was on a yo-yo string, bouncing back and forth between freedom and capture. I hadn't been out long from the last case before I got arrested in Colorado on another robbery charge. They didn't have a case, only this time I accepted a plea bargain for the robbery. Larry had brought in another guy called Dave Cross to do a robbery. I didn't even go into the place. I thought they had me on a pharmacy robbery, but it was a different one. A felony theft charge at the time could get you a maximum of 40 years, but instead they offered me a zip number. That's a Zero to 10 year sentence and I took it. My first stop in this new stretch was a maximum security facility in Canon City.

At Canon City, the guy at the top of the food chain was called The Captain (the head of the guards). I don't know if he was a captain in the military or the police, but that what everyone called him.

One day I got called to the Captain's office. It was like being called to the principal's office in school and I wondered what the hell I had done wrong. Well, I knew what I had done, I just didn't know what they'd caught me doing!

I walked over to the office and when I walked in the door, I was surprised to see a lot of the new prison friends I'd made sitting around the office, and the captain nowhere in sight. It didn't take me too long to figure out the situation. This was a collection of the guys running every racket in the place. There was a guy called Harpo and two brothers Doug and Mike who ran speed. Earl the heroin kingpin, and Frank the cook, along with a few other foot soldiers. After I sat down, Harpo explained that they wanted me to go into business with them. I already had my own hustle selling drugs on the inside and they respected the way I did business. They offered me a good deal, but they knew I was an independent. These guys weren't just the kingpins of the prison drug trade, they were still doing business on the outside too. They were drug kings, inside and outside of prison. I didn't go all in on the deal they were offering, but we still agreed to help each other out where we could. When I left that meeting, it took me a second to collect my thoughts. I'd seen some crazy shit on the inside but holding a secret meeting of the prison's biggest drug dealers in the Captain's office was something I never expected. This place might be even more fucked up than Lansing, which I realized would be very good for business.

A year later I was transferred to medium security where I was locked up from 1976 to '79. It was still part of the Canon City facility, but it was a section with a lower custody level. When I first got there, they assigned me to the trash truck. The job would allow me to go around the prison complex picking up trash. There were 7 prisons in Canon City at the time so it was a big job and allowed me and the other guys on trash detail a lot of opportunities to break the rules and acquire the supplies for my racket. How it would go down, is one of my friend's old lady would drop off the stuff in the trash outside of a home for battered women that was on our trash route. I would pick it up, smuggle it into the prison and give to one of the other guys in our crew. Once I handed it off to that guy, my job was done. It's was a pretty easy gig for 50% of the profits.

Every Thursday I would pick up the trash at the Canon City Women's Prison. We would eat lunch there and have a chat with the women; always with a lot of guards hanging around. It always seemed crazy to me. 15 guards for 60 Women and 2 men from medium security. That where I learned that women in prison absolutely hate women who abuse their kids. Even more than men do. And they will make a woman's life hell in there.

About 5 months in, the jig was up. Someone found out about my connection on the outside and they removed me from trash duty. Told me that I didn't work there anymore. It wasn't a big deal to me; wherever I went I could always find a way to make a living on the side. I was always hustling to get what I needed. With two kids on the streets outside, I had to do what I had to do. So after trash duty they moved me to the kitchen.

It didn't take long to find out that the guys in the kitchen were trying to figure out a way to break into the walk-in cooler. We were eating slop and the good grub for the guards and officers was behind lock and key. The inmates in the kitchen didn't know how it worked to be able to get into the walk in, but I had access to a crescent wrench, and the knowledge to get us in. We couldn't pick the lock but had the idea to take the crescent wrench and loosen the hinges, so we didn't even need to open the lock. I got my share of the take and also earned some respect from my new coworkers.

But I wasn't satisfied with just one scheme at a time. I had a friend who worked in the canteen and based on what he told me, I thought that their system for tracking sales would be easy to manipulate. They had a file for each inmate and at the end of each week they would add up your canteen and they would put the receipt in your file. My friend who worked in the Canteen would add mine and his, but it just so happened that our money totals would always stay the same. I hustled a scheme with 5 other guys to get half of whatever they got. They lost no money and got free canteen and I kicked up to my buddy who worked there.

Another scheme I had through the canteen was where you could make "downtown purchases" at the prison store. We had a connection at a local supermarket who would prepare certain items for sae at the canteen. A can of cocoa for instance. They would empty out that can, replace it with weed on the bottom, or whatever I wanted to smuggle in, and then add back in that cocoa and pack it down so it was undetectable. Then they would put two black dots on the can so the guy who would pick it up knew that it was "that can". There was a prisoner who would do the shopping and was a part of our scam to bring the stuff into the joint. Then we would go in to pick it up right under the guards noses. They had no clue, just thought we made a lot of hot chocolate.

In 1979 they let me out. I went back to Wichita, got a job and started working. My wife and I briefly got back together after I got back, but it wasn't long before she left with the kids again. After that I went back to a life of crime. I reconnected with an old friend named Tom and got starting running cars across the border to Mexico. I did alright for a while, but they arrested me at the border coming back into the country. They sent me to San Angelo and then dropped the charges 30 days later.

I went back to Colorado in 1980 and got back into the "steal business". Stealing from Money Mart and anywhere else I could find. The heat came down from hitting all the Money Marts and I ran to Arizona and holed up with another friend of mine. In Arizona, I started doing string robberies again and got busted and went to jail. They offered me 7 years with that robbery, so I took it. They extradited me back to Colorado where I already had a plea bargain and they gave me 6 years that ran concurrently with my Arizona sentence, then I went back to Arizona to serve my time.

One thing I've learned during my time in the system is that plea bargains are a poor man's justice; and public defenders are really just for the public. When you're talking to the cops be smart, don't tell them anything! They mean it when they say, "Anything you say can be used against you!"

In Arizona I was locked up in the State Prison in Florence and of course I was smuggling again. I was dealing what I called, "green and canteen". In Arizona, they measured their weed in "chap-caps", caps from a ChapStick containers. 10 dollars each or 3 for 25. I liked hash and the best hash cost 180 dollars for an ounce. Those 28 grams I could sell for 50 dollars each and make 1400 dollars. Or I could paper it out into smaller amounts and make more. It was kind of down to how much work I wanted to do.

I was about 3 years into my sentence, and they thought they had caught me. They called me into the Captain's office one day where a guy named Nye was in the office. He worked for Internal Investigations and he told me that they had found a photo album mailed to me that was full of drugs. He asked me what he thought they should do to me. What a dumb fucking question. I said, "Well, that's illegal, isn't it? You should probably prosecute me to the fullest extent of the law." He knew he had nothing on me and I knew it too.

I was sent to Cell Block 6 which at ASP was the hole and it's where I spent the next three and a half years. The guards beat me, did cavity searches and ground my food into a paste for my meals. I sued about the cavity searches and won $2000 in a settlement. When they put me in the hole, in CB6, I lost all of my good time without even getting a hearing. It's still crazy to me that you go through a trial to get put in prison in the first place, but if they want to keep you there, you don't even get a hearing.

Over my years in prison, I'd learned that the guards wouldn't mess with religion and would make exceptions for religious practices. Because of this, I converted to be a member of the Sikh Religion. They got special food to eat due to their beliefs and these exceptions helped me to survive in that hell hole!!

They really hated me! I really hated them! The cops had done about everything they could possibly do to me. What if I had done to them what I described above? They would call me an animal! I'd love to do some cavity searches on them! Make them eat shit! Why not?! Fuck those assholes!! Do onto others as they have done onto you!

I did my time in Arizona from 1980 to 1986. At that point I really thought I was done with the criminal life, but sometimes you just need one more taste and it cost me twenty more years of my life. I went back to Colorado and got busted for robbery again! In 1986, I was 38 years old, and they gave me 2 consecutive sentences of 16 years and a day for a total of 32 years.

After all that time in prison, I was getting pretty good at writing writs and filing motions. I had actually helped get a guy named Rick out of prison. He wanted to call a witness that was flying in and asked the judge for a continuance, but the motion was denied. He was my cell mate, so I took a look at his case and I wondered why his previous lawyer didn't see the errors I was noticing. I had Rick file a motion and based on the mishandling of his case by the judge, he got out. I told him, "in the kangaroo courts in prison they can do that shit, but they can't legally deny you a witness in court." I predicted that they were going to offer him time served and sure enough, he took it and was released.

The next 20 years they moved me from one prison to another. I was smuggling stuff inside the walls the whole time I was locked up, but I was never caught. In Colorado prisons the money options were canteen, green money and street to street. I would hustle a lot of canteen, but you could only hold 40 dollars, so I would spread the money around the prison and I'd trade the canteen for green money and street to street. On the streets I had a connection named Angie. I would give her a call about once a week and tell her where I wanted to money to go. She sent the money overnight and my connections on the other end sent weed back into the prison. I always tried to smuggle in the best. None of that Mexican brick weed. With a 200 dollar investment I could easily make 500 or 600 dollars. I also set things up for other dealers in exchange for 30 percent of their future sales. You could sell a matchbox packed full of weed back then for $50, then the next guy could break out that weed into 50 joints that sell for 2 bucks a piece and make some money on his end too.

Smuggling just became a way of life for me on the inside. I was talking to my competitor one day and he asked what the strangest thing was that I ever smuggled inside. I didn't remember anything too crazy, so I said steroids and he told me a friend had wanted him to smuggle in an inflatable woman.

I did 5 years in Canon City and then was moved to Ordway, Colorado. I served 5 years there and then did another 5 years in Limon. One morning about halfway through my five years at Limon I woke up with a terrible stomach pain and I went to the medical officer where they put me on a gurney and left me there all day waiting for treatment. Around 10 o'clock at night I was loaded up for transport to Denver General Hospital. I was in agony as I was handcuffed, shackled and belted in the van and then we waited another half hour inside the prison waiting for a maintenance worker to fix the broken gate.

The highway from Limon to Denver was bumpy and every bump sent a bolt of pain through my abdomen. When I got to the hospital it was Saturday night around midnight. I was on a gurney waiting for my blood test results and across from me there was a man who was a gunshot victim. The results came back and I was rushed into surgery with a burst appendix. I stayed in the hospital for 3 weeks and the doctors and nurses said I was lucky to be alive. I didn't necessarily feel that way. The prospect of going back to prison for another 10 years was staring me in the face. The room I was in wasn't like a civilian hospital, it was more like a cell with metal bars and bulletproof glass for windows. Even outside of prison, there were still constant reminders that I was still trapped. It took me three weeks before I could walk 30 feet and eat a piece of sponge cake, but once I could walk and eat, I was taken back to Limon.

Around 1997 or so, I started to see the parole board. I knew I wouldn't ever make parole and they knew it too, but they were obligated to give me my day in court. I got denied in 1997 and I went to the board again in 2000. A parole board member named Don Alders was there and it was obvious to me that he had had a few nips before the hearing. Come to find out, while I am at my hearing, Alders is having his car detailed by prisoners. Which is a government car to boot. They found alcohol in the front of his car and the convict that was cleaning the car at the time refused to finish because he didn't want to be charged for the alcohol in a government vehicle. The guard on duty called the warden who told Alders to get off of the property. Driving into the prison there was a big sign that states when you drive into any prison that past that point you could not have Alcohol, Drugs, Ammunition. But of course, they did nothing to him!!

At the next parole hearing a year later, a guy named Larry Schwartz was on the board. I saw a story in the Denver Post a few years later that he was accused of molesting his daughter. They couldn't charge him due the statute of limitations, but he was taken off the parole board. They fired the child molester but kept the drunk Alders.

The next year, I sent my parole plan into the White House! I thought it would be a good joke to send an appeal to the President - I figured he was about as likely to give me my freedom as the parole board was. At my hearing that year, they asked me if I thought it was funny. I replied, "Yeah, it is! It's about as funny as Don Alders illegally bringing booze onto state property! But he is special!!!" These law breakers on my parole board thought they were all so special. They thought they were better men than all of us that stood in front of them, but they were dead wrong.

In 2001 I was sent to Sterling, Colorado where I was held for another 5 years. In Sterling they had what we called the "death fence". When you first go into the prison, while you're still in quarantine, the guard shows you a video about this fence. That when I learned that the first touch of the fence hits you with about 500 volts of electricity; the second touch hits you with 5,000 volts! The first time you touch it, it will shock you. The next time you touch it, it will kill you! We knew they weren't lying because when raindrops hit the fence, they would pop and sizzle. Birds that landed on the fence got cooked alive. And he did escape. After scouting out the fence for a while, I told my friend Doug that I had a plan of how to beat the fence. There was an area with a gate where it was washed out and I thought you could put a leather floor mat around your body as you crawled under the area that was electrified. The only problem was that it wouldn't work in maximum security, one of us would have to get a lower custody area of the prison. It took him about a year to get there, but once he did, Doug took my advice and he escaped. He eventually got caught a day or so later in Wray, Colorado, but everyone was amazed that he had escaped from the prison where everyone thought that was impossible.

Life in prison was still violent and there were still scary moments, but I had become numb to a lot of the situations that used to scare me. I was in the chow hall at Sterling and a couple of guys were arguing about a stolen cassette tape player. They didn't care about playing music, prisoners would make tattoo guns out of the cassette motors. The guy who stole the player was wearing glasses and the owner of the player hit him in the face, breaking his glasses and leaving pieces of glass in his face and eyes. This started a bigger fight and then came the guards and the teargas. And I just I kept eating through it all. I knew we would be locked down for a while and wouldn't be getting food so I ate as fast as I could with the teargas in the air.

A year later, I go to the parole board again. This time, I saw an old man sitting on the parole board. I asked him, "Are you a drunk, or a child molester, or both?!" He was surprised and he said, "What are you talking about?!" So I told him about what happened with Don Alders and Larry Schwarz. I said, "If you don't believe me, ask my case manager!" My case manager confirmed my story, but it didn't help me one bit. Another set off of my parole, of course.

In 2005 I'd done almost 20 years and I was take to Cheyenne Mountain Center, which is a re-entry Center. I did 6 months there before finally getting my freedom. Most of my freedom at least.

I still hadn't been given parole, but I was offered to be put in an Intensive Supervision Program. They put an ankle monitor on me and I got a job as a Telemarketer. After 3 years on the monitor, they finally offered me parole for the last two years of my sentence. I told them, No! After all that time in prison, I knew the law pretty well. I knew that if I took parole, I'd have to pay for the ankle monitor, and pay for the substance abuse prevention classes, and I'd still have report to a parole officer. My time with ISP allowed me the same freedom, but they would have to continue to pay for it. It felt like I finally won a victory against the system.

I finally got a discharge in 2011. After 25 years for robbery, they finally discharged me. I did a total of 36 years in prison and 5 on an ankle monitor.

The last story I'll tell happened when I was in Sterling, around 2004. I had to go to the hospital to meet a doctor about removing my gall bladder and when I returned, they didn't have a cell open in my pod. They ended up putting me in C Pod until I could get back to my normal cell and while I was in C Pod I met Timothy Masters. They needed a 4th guy for "Pea knuckle" and I sat down with some guys I recognized, but didn't really know. I only knew Masters by reputation. I'd heard from other inmates that he was always saying he was innocent and that they actually believed him. I really didn't care. As long as he wasn't a rapist or pedophile, he was just another guy to me. A lot of people say they are framed or innocent in prison, whatever.

Masters ended up doing a total of 10 years. When I met him, he had only been in for about a couple of years and after 10 years he was granted an appeal in a highly publicized case. After new evidence was brought to light, Masters was released immediately and all of the charges were dropped.

Masters eventually hired a lawyer who filed a suit against the State of Colorado and won Masters $10 Million Dollars on the condition that the state would admit no wrongdoing! Imagine, how much they would have offered if they DID do something wrong! This is just par for the course. This stuff happens all of the time in the criminal justice system and there is just hardly any proof. That's OUR SYSTEM Ladies and Gentleman! Take or Leave it.

"Oho!" they cried, "The world is wide,

But fettered limbs, go lame!

And once, or twice, to throw the dice

Is a gentlemanly game,

But he does not win who plays with Sin

In the secret House of Shame."

~Oscar Wilde~ 1854-1900